writing guides

ACTIVITIE

Explanations

HUW THOMAS

NON-FICTION FOR AGES 9–11

CONTENTS

INTRODUCTION

The Scholastic *Writing Guides* series provides teachers with ideas and projects that promote a range of writing, bringing insights from educational research into the classroom. Each guide explores a different type of writing and provides example material, background information, photocopiable activities and teaching suggestions. Their aim is to enable teachers to guide the writing process, share planning ideas and develop themes as a context for writing activities.

The materials:
- motivate children with interesting activities
- break complex types of writing into manageable teaching units
- focus on and develop the typical features of particular types of writing
- provide original approaches to teaching.

Each book is divided into sections, beginning with examples of the type of writing being taught. These are followed by ideas for developing writing and projects that will extend over a series of sessions.

SECTION ONE: USING GOOD EXAMPLES

Section One looks at good examples of the genre, with the emphasis on using texts to stimulate and develop writing. Two example texts are shared, and questions that focus the discussion on their significant features are suggested. This is followed by activities that explore what the texts can teach us about writing, enabling teachers to compare the two texts and to go on to model the type of writing presented in the guide.

SECTION TWO: DEVELOPING WRITING

Section Two moves from reading to writing. This section provides activities that prompt and support children in planning and writing. A range of approaches includes planning templates and strategies to stimulate ideas. The activities refine children's ideas about the type of writing being developed and give them focused writing practice in the context of scaffolded tasks. Teacher's notes support each activity by explaining the objective and giving guidance on delivery.

SECTION THREE: WRITING

Section Three moves on to writing projects. Building upon the earlier work in Section Two, these projects aim to develop the quality of writing and provide a selection of ideas for class or group work on a particular theme or idea. The teacher may choose to use some or all of the ideas presented in each project as a way of weaving the strategies developed in Section Two into a more complex and extended writing task.

SECTION FOUR: REVIEW

Section Four supports the assessment process. Children are encouraged to reflect on the type of writing they are tackling and to evaluate how effectively their work has met the criteria for the genre identified in Section One.

How it works

A car engine is called an 'internal combustion engine', because the movement is caused by the combustion (burning) of fuel *inside* the engine.

The engine contains a set of cylinders. A valve at the top of each cylinder lets in a mixture of petrol and air known as a 'charge'. Once the charge is in the cylinder, a spark plug ignites it – causing a small explosion. This explosion pushes a piston down, pulling a weight attached to the piston upwards.

A second valve lets the burnt petrol and air mixture out of the cylinder, and the weight starts to push down. Consequently, the piston goes back up. Another charge enters the cylinder and ignites: down goes the piston, up goes the weight – then out blow the gases, down goes the weight and up goes the piston again.

A component called the distributor sends a spark to each cylinder at just the right time. Sometimes an engine needs tuning to make sure this works.

The piston is connected to a crankshaft. This has the effect of turning an up-and-down movement into a turning-round movement, a bit like a leg turning a pedal on a bike. The circular movement is then transmitted to the car's wheels – so the car moves.

All car engines have cylinders to burn the petrol and turn the crankshafts. Most have four cylinders, but some have six or more. The burnt gases leave the engine, and are emitted from the exhaust at the back of the car.

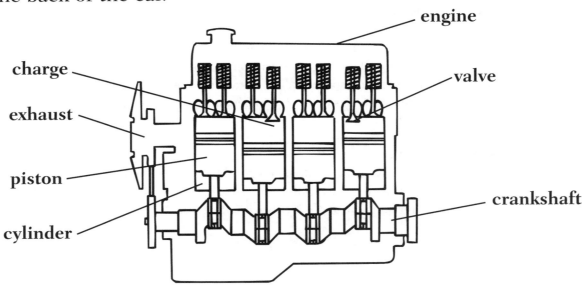

writing guides: EXPLANATIONS

Encyclopedia entries

Why does the sea have waves?

Waves on the sea are caused by the wind. Inside a wave, the water particles go round in a spiral, like the cars in a roller-coaster. The waves become taller as the wind blows them across the sea. As the waves approach the shore, the water becomes shallower. The sea bed interferes with the spiral movement of the water particles, causing the waves to topple over or 'break' on the shore.

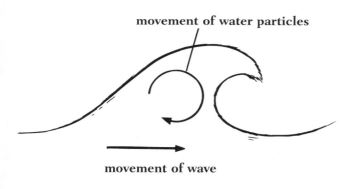

movement of water particles

movement of wave

Why does a metal ship float?

A solid lump of metal will sink in water – but a ship whose body or hull is made from metal can float because it is hollow. The water pushes up on the ship with a force called upthrust. The bigger the surface in contact with the water, the bigger the upthrust. This is why ships are wide and flattened underneath. Because the inside of the ship is full of air, its total weight is not enough to overcome the upthrust – so the ship floats. If the bottom or keel were completely flat, the ship would float even better – but it would be much harder to steer.

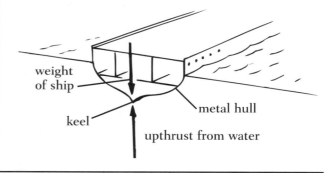

weight of ship

keel

metal hull

upthrust from water

Why do we brush our teeth?

We brush our teeth to stop them decaying. Our teeth are protected by a hard layer called enamel. Fragments of food caught on our teeth form a sticky coating called plaque in which bacteria can breed – especially when the food contains sugar. The bacteria attack the enamel surface of the tooth and make a hole or cavity in the softer core, leading to tooth decay. When the decay reaches the nerves in the tooth, the pain starts! Regular brushing keeps plaque off our teeth and so keeps the enamel layer intact.

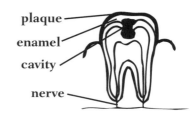

plaque

enamel

cavity

nerve

SECTION ONE
USING GOOD EXAMPLES

To explain something, we say why or how it has happened. An explanation text is an account of a process. It shows the steps in a process, one thing causing another, and so explains the outcome. It may refer to past events, the workings of social processes (such as elections), scientific models (such as the atom) or abstract concepts (such as force).

In this section, a detailed explanation is given of a process that has a lot of interest for this age group and will support work on forces: the mechanism of a car engine. This example is supported by three shorter explanations that might appear as entries in a science encyclopedia.

Shared activities

How it works
Before you read this text, ask the children what they know about cars and how they work. You may find they know a lot: that an engine moves the car, the engine is fuelled by petrol and so on. Note what they say on a board or flip chart. Now ask them to list what they would like to know about the workings of a car.

Read 'How it works' together, then look back at the things the children wanted to know. Have any of these questions been answered? Point out the use of technical vocabulary in the text, circling any examples the children can pick out. Focus on the use of the present tense in this text. Unless it is explaining a specific past event, an explanation usually refers to a process as if it were happening at that moment (*A valve… lets in a mixture of petrol and air; This explosion pushes a piston…*).

Ask the children to create a flow diagram showing the process described in the text. This should not be a technical diagram, just a simple outline of the steps in the process by which the car works (with an arrow linking each step to the next).

Ask the children to re-read the text, looking for examples of one thing causing or being caused by another. Can they find the words used to show these connections?

Many explanation texts use diagrams to show the process they explain. Look at the diagram on page 4 and check how well it supports the explanation. Does it help to show the stages of the process?

Encyclopedia entries
Read the three entries and look at the similar features of each text. They all have the same function of answering a question; they all give stages in a process leading to the outcome they explain; and they are all written in the present tense.

Ask the children to read through each explanation, then try partitioning it into three or four distinct stages. A wave breaks, a boat floats and a tooth decays – but what stages make up each process? The children should work in groups of three or four, with each group dividing an explanation into stages, noting them down and then sharing them with the class. Encourage them to represent each process by a flow chart, with the stages linked by arrows. If you are projecting the photocopiable sheet, you could add numbers to each entry to show the stages in each process.

Finally, discuss the way in which explanation texts often summarise a process and then go through it in more detail. Use both shared texts to illustrate this. Discuss how an explanation states the cause of something we observe by referring to previous events (such as a wave starting in mid-ocean), invisible things (such as bacteria) or abstract ideas (such as upthrust). Consider some examples of unsatisfactory explanations, such as: *A metal ship floats because it produces an anti-sinking force.*

Taking ideas further

Stress to the children that, as they read these texts, they are learning how to write explanations. This means that they should try to identify the content and style features of good explanations. Can they see how explanations help us to make sense of the world? In the three activities that follow, read the instruction at the top of the sheet to the children.

Techni-questions

Scientific explanations are shared: scientists read them in one text and rewrite them in another. This activity puts children in the same position. Having read the text on page 4, they use it as a basis for their own explanations. Cut up the questions on page 8 and give them to different pairs of children, who read them to the rest of the group. The group try to answer the questions without looking at the text. The two 'questioners' listen to the answers and decide whether they are hearing a clear and thorough answer. If not, they should push for a bit more explanation. Finally, the group re-read the text – does this change their answers?

Explain the word

A significant aspect of an explanation is the fitting of technical material into a pattern. A process such as engine mechanics is presented step by step, so that it can be understood more easily. In this activity, the children investigate some of the technical terms used in the three encyclopaedia entries on photocopiable page 5. Organise the children into groups of three or four, preferably of mixed ability. Give each group a copy of page 5 and one cut-out word from page 9. Their task is to read the word, say what they think it means and make a note of this on a sheet of paper. They should then swap with another group who have finished, keeping the activity moving along. When most of the groups have tackled most of the words, call the children back together and decide on a shared definition of each word.

We want the details!

An explanation clarifies a superficial or *prima facie* fact, such as *It rains* or *Cars move*, by stating the reasons behind it. To do this, it needs to include details of the process. In this activity, the children are given simply worded facts and asked to flesh out some of the detail behind them.

Cut out each cloud from page 10 and stick it in the centre of an A3 sheet of paper. Each small group can take one sheet of paper (if you like, the whole class can work on a few of these first). The children should point to words that they could question in order to provide more detail. For example, with *Pistons can turn car wheels*, the children could point to the word *Pistons* and ask *How does it do that?*, then say *A crankshaft transmits the force*. Because they have encountered these processes in the shared texts, the children will be able to judge where these sentences are vague and what details will clarify them. They should end up with an A3 page covered in questions, with detailed answers, radiating out from the cloud.

Explanation writing

Photocopy page 11 to A3 size. This chart uses features the children have encountered in their shared reading to help them develop their own explanation writing. It quotes examples from the shared texts, and gives questions that will stimulate new writing. The chart can also be used to help children evaluate explanation texts by seeing how they match the criteria given. It should be displayed while the children are writing their explanations.

Techni-questions

Here are some technical questions. Can you answer them?
Each question requires you to explain something.

How can petrol make wheels move?

What happens inside an engine cylinder?

What causes a piston in an engine to move?

Why do cars produce exhaust fumes?

Why are car engines called internal combustion engines?

How do the little explosions in an engine happen?

Explain the word

Can you explain what each of these words means? Use the three encyclopedia entries to help you.

float	upthrust
decay	plaque
bacteria	enamel
interfere	hollow
particles	shallow

We want the details!

These explanations are true, but they don't tell us very much.
Can you develop them into fuller explanations?

Petrol makes a car go.

Pistons turn car wheels.

Waves break when they reach the shore.

A ship floats by pushing water.

Teeth are helped by brushing.

writing guides: **EXPLANATIONS**

Explanation writing

Remember...	For example...	When planning, ask yourself...
Show the **how** or **why** of something.	Why does a boat float on water?	What **how** or **why** question am I answering?
Describe a step-by-step process.	Charge ➡ spark ➡ explosion ➡ piston down ➡ weight lifted	What are the stages in this process?
Use time connectives for **when** each step happens.	'**Then** the tooth develops a cavity.'	Have I used words that describe a sequence in time?
Use causal connectives for what causes what.	'The shape of the boat **means** that...'	How did one thing cause another?
Use the simple present tense.	'Bacteria multiply...'	Is my writing set in the present?
Use technical vocabulary.	cylinder, piston, crankshaft	Have I used accurate terms?
Add a diagram if it will be helpful.	a diagram of a tooth	Will a diagram make the explanation clearer?

Writing an explanation – whether in science or in another subject area, such as art or politics – involves outlining the process behind something that we observe. As such, all explanations have a sequential structure in which one thing causes another. The process of writing explanations needs to reflect this structure. The paragraphing of such texts is often based on the steps in a process. An explanation needs to use connecting language: the language of time, and of cause and effect. The activities in this section explore ways in which children can consider cause and effect and the steps in a process when writing their own explanatory texts.

ARROWS

WHAT YOU NEED

Photocopiable page 16, a selection of games (commercial or home-made) with a science or technology element, writing materials.

WHAT TO DO

The recording of how one thing is caused by or follows another is a key aspect of explanation writing. To start this activity, ask the children to look at how one thing leads to another in some well-known games. Examples such as the way the kipper is flipped in 'Flip the kipper', the routine for 'Pass the parcel', the way the marbles fall in 'Kerplunk!' or how the trap is sprung in 'Mousetrap' all involve chains of linked events. Ask the children to record the specific stages of a game using photocopiable page 16: between the arrows, they should write descriptions of the stages. They could use temporal or causal connectives. (The latter are especially significant, and should be encouraged.)

Widen the discussion to include explanations of processes in technology (how something works) or science (outlining a natural process). Agree on a suitable process (such as the water cycle or the working of a fountain) for the children to explain, using another copy of page 16. Once they have completed an 'arrows' explanation, the children can record some of the connective words they have used by writing them above the arrows. Finally, they can use the notes they have made on the sheet to write a short explanation text about their subject.

CAUSE AND EFFECT

WHAT YOU NEED

Photocopiable page 17 copied onto card, scissors, glue, paper, writing materials.

WHAT TO DO

Page 17 presents a set of broken-up sentences in which each clause describes a cause or an effect. Ask the children to work in pairs, cutting out the ten cards and shuffling them, then sorting them into causes and effects. Can they fit the pairs together by identifying the process being explained in each sentence? Point out the connecting words used to start the 'effect' clauses. Ask the children to make a list of these words.

Now ask the children to remove all the effects (the second clauses) and shuffle the causes (the first clauses). Can they read each first clause and provide their own second clause, using their own words, then write out the whole explanatory sentence? They can refer to their list of connective words to help them. Then they can rebuild the earlier sentences and compare these with their own versions.

LINK CHALLENGE

WHAT YOU NEED

Photocopiable page 18, three or four reference books for each group, writing materials.

WHAT TO DO

Ask the children to work in groups of three, with individual copies of page 18 and a few reference books covering subject matter with which the children are familiar. These could be machines they have studied, or areas of the science or geography curriculum. For each connective word on page 18, the children need to devise a sentence in which that word links the first clause to the second clause. The connective words are either causal (one thing is caused by or causes another: *because, so, as a result, therefore*) or temporal (linking events over time: *then, next, after*).

The children can use the textbooks to prompt the subject matter for their explanatory sentences, for example: *Rain falls from the sky after water in the clouds condenses* or *A roundabout in a fairground moves because a crank turns a gear*. Each group should try to fill three sheets with different sentences.

OPENING STATEMENTS

WHAT YOU NEED

Photocopiable page 19.

WHAT TO DO

An explanation often begins with an opening statement that introduces the rest of the text by summarising what will be said, for example: *A car engine looks very complicated, but it works using simple physical principles*.

In this activity, the children do not need to write an explanation. They just need to decide what 'how' or 'why' question they could answer and create an appropriate opening sentence. Their sentence should introduce the topic in broad terms. The children can choose topics from their current work across the curriculum or from their own interests. For example, if they were explaining why spiders make webs, they could write: *Spiders make complex webs to stay alive* or *A web is the way spiders catch their food*. Remind them to use verbs in the simple present tense (*make, get* and so on), indicating a process that is happening continually.

QUESTIONING

WHAT YOU NEED

Photocopiable page 20, large sheets of paper, writing materials.

WHAT TO DO

The children should work on this activity independently before forming groups, perhaps as part of an expanded plenary session. Ask them to read the four facts printed on the left-hand side of page 20 and think of two questions they would like to ask about each fact. For example: for *The sun rises in the morning*, the children might ask *Where does it come from?* or *Why does it rise?*

When they have filled in the sheet, the children should form groups of four to six and decide which fact has provoked the biggest number of different questions. They should write this fact on a large sheet of paper, with the questions around it. Discuss with the children what explanations might answer these questions. Lead them to understand that an explanation is always answering a question.

writing guides: **EXPLANATIONS**

OBJECTIVE

■ To plan a written explanation.

PLANNING AND DISCUSSING
WHAT YOU NEED

Photocopiable page 21 copied onto card, scissors, paper, writing materials.

WHAT TO DO

The children should work in groups of three. Each group needs to cut out the question cards from a copy of page 21, shuffle them and lay them out face down. They take turns to pick up two cards each, then work individually to plan a short explanatory answer for each of their two questions. Their planning should be structured around the steps in a process, exploring how one thing leads to another.

Ask the children to make notes for their explanations. These could be simple written notes or diagrams with arrows. Once each member of the group has completed two plans, they can reconvene and share their outcomes. This might be done in a later lesson, as at least ten minutes needs to be allowed for planning. The children should take turns to share the plan they think they have written most clearly with the rest of their group. The group can evaluate and comment on each other's planning. Was anything left out? Were the events described in the right order?

Finally, the trio need to agree which of the three plans they will follow through to a complete explanation. They should then each write an explanatory text dealing with the same question, following a final plan to which they have all contributed.

OBJECTIVE

■ To organise an explanatory text.

CHOCOLATE CHANGES
WHAT YOU NEED

Photocopiable page 22, a bar of chocolate, a large sheet of paper, a marker pen.

WHAT TO DO

This activity needs some preparation on a previous day. Ask the children whether they have ever left some chocolate in a warm place. *What happened?* Take a bar of chocolate and leave it in a warm place, such as a sunny window-ledge or a shelf near a radiator. Return a few hours later to see what has happened. The bar will have melted. Now leave it in a cool place and return a few hours later. The bar will have solidified again. Discuss this process with the children, prompting them to ask questions about it. They might ask why or how the chocolate changes. Any such questions should be recorded (in note form) on a shared sheet of paper.

On a later day, give the children copies of page 22. Ask them to number the chocolate squares in the correct order to explain the changes. When they have done this, ask them to write the first three words from each square on a separate sheet of paper. Let them re-read the explanation text. Now ask them to write down three technical words used in the text (such as *particles* or *solid*) and consider whether the text answers the questions listed earlier. Finally, ask them to cut out the picture rectangles from the chocolate squares and keep these for the follow-up activity.

In a later lesson, they can use the questions, sentence starters, technical vocabulary and pictures as a basis for writing an explanation of the chocolate changes. They should try to answer all of their questions in their explanation text. The explanation should have an opening sentence that summarises what will be said.

HOW AND WHY KWL CHART
WHAT YOU NEED

Photocopiable page 23, research materials (such as reference books, CD-ROMs and the Internet), writing materials, paper.

writing guides: **EXPLANATIONS**

WHAT TO DO

A 'KWL chart' is used to gather information. It provides an effective way of matching questions to investigation and writing activities. KWL charts were invented by DM Ogle (in *Children's Comprehension of Text* edited by K Denise Muth) to provide active ways in which children could develop a research process.

To employ a KWL chart in explanation writing, use an enlarged copy of page 23. Talk through the column headings with the children, pointing out how the words *Know*, *Want* and *Learned* make the initials KWL. Guide the children through the task of filling in the first column by listing what they already know about a topic in note form. For example, if you pick the topic 'How our country is ruled', they may know that the Government is decided by an election every few years.

The next column provides a space for the children to suggest what they would like to find out. They may ask questions such as *What is a Government?* or *Is the Prime Minister in charge?* However, to prompt explanatory writing, you need to encourage them to ask questions that start with *How* or *Why*, for example: *How are laws decided?* or *Why are there so many MPs?* Research that stems from these questions will provide suitable material for writing explanations.

Follow this up with group work on researching the subject. The children can make notes to answer their questions. Bring the groups together and agree on answers to be recorded in the final column, as well as the children's thoughts about areas that could be explored further.

OBJECTIVE
■ To structure explanation writing around investigative questions.

K What we **know**	W What we **want** to find out	L What we have **learned** or still need to learn
MPs are Members of Parliament.	Why are there so many?	There is one for each constituency (area of the country).
People vote in elections.	How do people vote?	General Elections have to be held at least every five years.
	What do the votes achieve?	A local candidate is elected as a Member of Parliament.

PRONOUNS

WHAT YOU NEED

Explanatory texts (see 'What to do'), paper, writing materials, board or flip chart.

WHAT TO DO

When writing non-fiction texts, children need to switch between using nouns and using pronouns, for example: *The Sun heats up the water. As it becomes warmer, it evaporates faster*. In this example, there is some ambiguity in the use of the pronoun: *it* refers to the water, but grammatically *it* could refer to the Sun. In this activity, the children look at the way that pronouns often stand in for nouns.

Ask the children to look at an explanatory text. This could be an explanation from section 1 (page 4 or 5), but ideally it should be one they have produced in their own science writing or taken from a textbook they have used. Ask them to read the text carefully, looking for pronouns. Each child should fold a sheet of blank paper down the middle, then work with a partner to make a list of all the pronouns they can find in the text. These should be listed on the left-hand side of their folded sheet. Each pronoun should be listed as many times as it occurs.

Now the children should revisit each pronoun, looking at what it referred to in the text and record this on the right-hand side of the sheet. Because of the way that such texts are structured, the pronouns often refer to an object in a previous sentence as it continues to feature in the process being explained. Encourage the children to think of this as being like the baton in a relay race: the pronoun carries the object forward into the next clause or sentence.

Finally, ask the children to check whether it is clear what each pronoun refers to. Note any examples of ambiguity on the board, and discuss how they could be rewritten to make them clear.

OBJECTIVE
■ To evaluate the clarity of pronoun use in explanatory texts.

writing guides: **EXPLANATIONS**

Arrows

Use this flow chart to make an explanation by recording how
one thing leads to another.

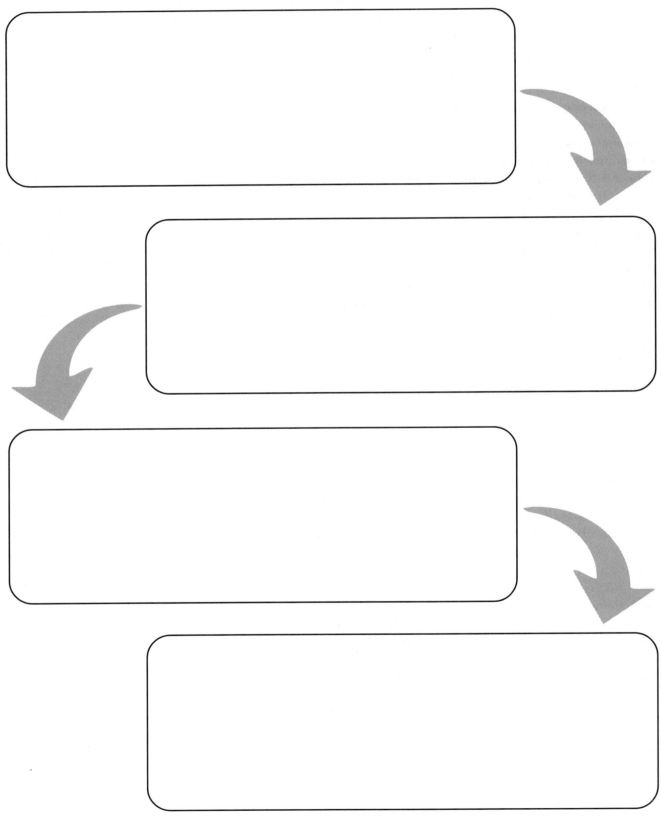

Cause and effect

Join up the pairs of causes and effects.

The Sun warms a puddle,

because heat from the flame melts the wax.

The particles in a liquid move freely,

because its particles are held strongly together.

A candle melts

when it is heated.

A solid has a fixed shape

so water evaporates more quickly from the surface.

A solid may turn into a liquid

and consequently a liquid has no fixed shape.

Link challenge

Write two-part sentences using these linking words.

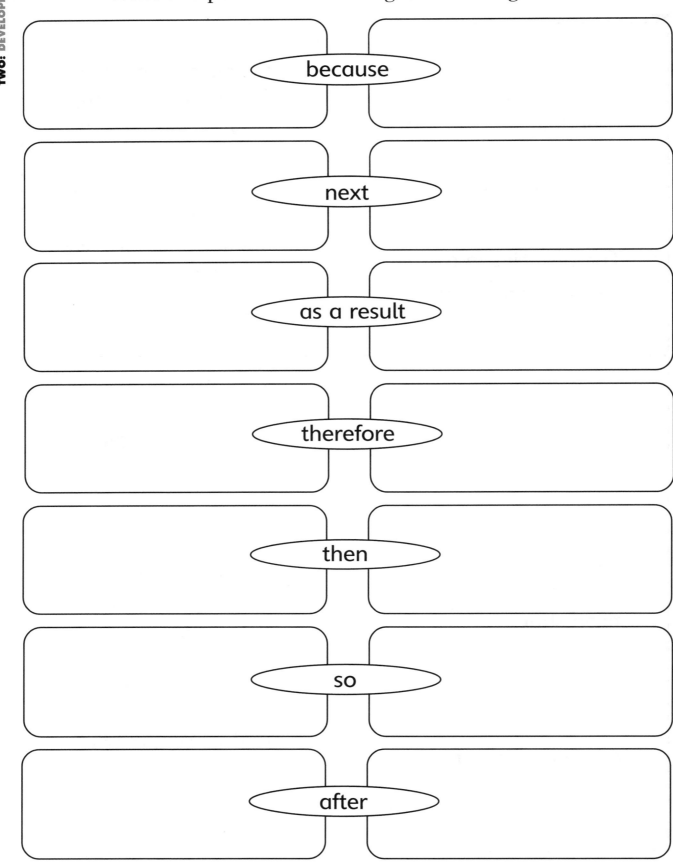

because

next

as a result

therefore

then

so

after

writing guides: **EXPLANATIONS**

Opening statements

Complete this table by writing opening statements for explanations.

In an explanation about...	I would answer the question...	An opening sentence could be...

Questioning

Can you think of two questions to ask about each fact?

The Sun rises in the morning.

Some birds fly south in the winter.

Wax melts when a candle burns.

Cars run out of petrol.

writing guides: **EXPLANATIONS**

Planning and discussing

Can you explain these things?

Why do we need shoelaces?

How does a bicycle work?

Why do puddles evaporate?

How does an ink stamp work?

Why are paper clips so useful?

Why do games need rules?

Chocolate changes

Number these sentences in the correct order. Then use them to write an explanation of how chocolate changes when it is first heated and then cooled.

A chocolate bar is solid.

Consequently the chocolate becomes solid again.

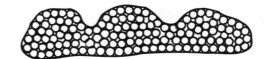

So the chocolate becomes runny and melts, changing into a liquid.

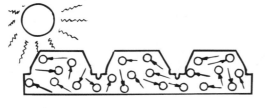

This is because the particles in the chocolate are held firmly together.

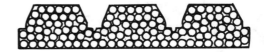

If chocolate becomes hot, the particles in it move about more freely.

If heat is then taken out of the liquid, the particles stop moving.

How and why KWL chart

K What we **know**	**W** What we **want** to find out	**L** What we have **learned** or still need to learn

SECTION THREE
WRITING

We have looked at examples of explanation texts and strategies for developing the writing of these texts. This section provides two writing projects in which children can engage with the process of explanation. Both projects involve the children being given written and pictorial information (in photocopied form) to go with first-hand experience of a process. These examples relate to a natural process (science) and the working of a mechanism (technology), but similar explanations could be written to explain a social process (citizenship), a writing process (literacy) or a data-handling process (mathematics).

In addition, a general 'Explanation planner' is provided. In both of the writing projects, this planner needs to be kept in mind. Copies can be filled in by the children, and a blank copy displayed as a wall poster.

Water writing

Photocopiable page 25 contains the kind of notes that children might gather after collating scientific information about the water cycle from a range of sources. The children should use these materials to help them write an explanation of the processes by which water passes through the water cycle. They may have other reference materials to hand that they have obtained in science or geography work, and it could be useful for them to widen the scope of their knowledge by referring to these.

Before writing, the children need to make notes structured around the water cycle. They should include: (a) an opening sentence to explain the subject; (b) a plan of the explanation (perhaps in the form of a flow chart), with the content of each paragraph in note form. Having done this, they can write an explanation of the water cycle – as a text alone or as an illustrated poster.

Clothes peg

Before they look at a text or plan any writing, give each child a clothes peg. Ask the children to think through how these marvellous machines work: how simple they are, and yet how useful we find them. Now ask them to read the 'Lever' and 'Spring' sections on photocopiable pages 26–7, then look at the questions and make notes for responses. They should then label the diagram, explaining what each part of a clothes peg does. Finally, the cycle diagram should act as a stimulus for structuring their explanation. They should make notes for an answer to the question *How do clothes pegs work?* They will need to explain what happens in each stage of the process. Ask them to consider questions such as: *What is the purpose of the spring? How does the peg exert leverage?* When they have made notes, ask them to write out their explanation text in full.

Explanation planner

The A3 photocopiable sheet on pages 28–9 provides a basis for preparing any explanatory text. Suitable examples will emerge from work in science, geography, technology and so on. The planner begins with a statement of the text's purpose: the question it needs to answer. The children should develop this by exploring key vocabulary and asking questions about the subject. A set of key general questions for any explanation are provided (elsewhere on the poster) to support this.

The main part of the planning process is the mapping out of the explanation in the form of a flow chart, with the stages linked by arrows. This structure models the explanation on the structure of the process to be explained. For example: the plan for an explanation of the water cycle would be presented in a cyclical form.

Finally, a simple planning frame provides space for the child to write the opening sentence of the text, outline three sections and then add a short conclusion.

writing guides: **EXPLANATIONS**

Water writing

Something you asked a geographer:

How do clouds make rain?

Rain is made by water in a cloud condensing from water vapour to liquid droplets. As the droplets get bigger, they turn into raindrops.

A reminder from your teacher:

Remember!
1. Rivers often flow between mountains.
2. Water is affected by gravity.

Notes from a TV programme you watched:

Water: collects ➡ rivers.
If water goes down through rocks + soil ➡ might join underground stream.

Three bits from an encyclopedia:

A water molecule can remain in the air for ten days before falling to the ground in a raindrop.

In clouds, small water droplets join together to make bigger drops.

Most rain falls over the sea. When water falls from the sky (as rain, hail, sleet or snow), this is called precipitation.

Something you read on a CD-ROM:

Heat from the Sun causes water to evaporate, turning it into a gas called water vapour. Water vapour rises. The higher it goes the colder it becomes, so it turns back into droplets of water. These droplets form clouds.

Word list on the classroom wall:

Evaporation

Condensation

Precipitation

Clothes peg

What do the different parts of a clothes peg do?

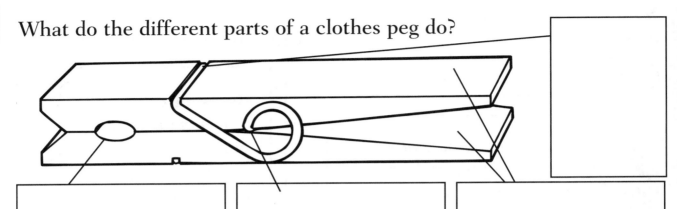

Lever

A lever is a simple machine that makes it easier to move something. It has a **load**, a **fulcrum** and an **effort**.

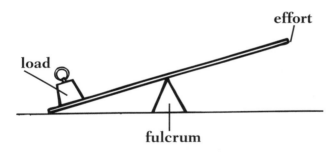

The **fulcrum** is the fixed point around which the lever turns. The **effort** is the force doing the moving. The **load** is the force that has to be moved.

If the arm to which the effort is applied is longer than the arm bearing the load, it is easier to move the load. The longer the effort arm is, the easier it is to move the load.

Spring

A spring is a piece of material, often metal, that is shaped in a particular way.

A spring can be either stretched or compressed, but it will tend to go back to its original shape. So it pulls when stretched and pushes when compressed.

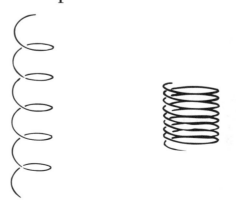

Questions about a clothes peg

Read and think about these.

What is the load being levered?

Why is the part you pinch so long?

Why is the wood (or plastic) the shape it is?

What are the holes for?

How does the spring connect to the lever?

Where is the fulcrum of the lever?

How a clothes peg works

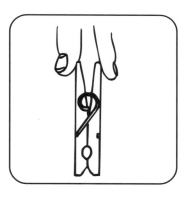

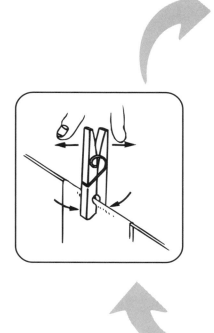

Explanation planner

The purpose of this explanation is to answer the question:

Glossary

What specialist terms will you use? Write their definitions.

Questions you have about this subject

writing guides: **EXPLANATIONS**

Map out the process

Plot the stages in the process you are explaining
by drawing a diagram. Here are three examples:

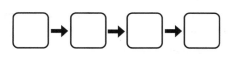 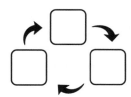 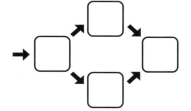

Some key questions

What is being
changed?

What is causing the
change?

What are the stages
in this change?

How does the
change start?

How does it end?

Plan your writing

Opening

a)

b)

c)

Conclusion

---

writing guides: **EXPLANATIONS**

SECTION FOUR
REVIEW

Why do explanations matter? Why do we read them?

This section applies these two questions to the writing tasks in the preceding sections. The children are asked to revisit their work, looking at how well their texts have explained a process, the links they have made and the vocabulary they have used. Emphasis is placed on sharing this task and comparing different explanations, thus helping the children to appreciate two ways in which they can improve their texts: by comparing different attempts and by gauging the response of readers. This underlines the point that explanations need to be agreed and shared between people if they are to be effective.

Read another

Ask the children to work in pairs. They should swap explanation texts and talk through the writing they have done. Each child should use photocopiable page 31 to assess his or her partner's explanation. The child should be able to see a clear process being outlined, specialist vocabulary, temporal and/or causal connections, and a change taking place within the process.

A successful explanation should set out to demystify its subject. It should be able to summarise in a phrase or sentence the process or event that is being explained. This is usually outlined in the first sentence of an explanatory text, so that the reader is given a clear indication of what the explanation will convey. If it isn't there, adding it might be suggested for a redraft.

The specialist vocabulary used should always be defined somewhere in the text. Again, if it isn't, this can be added in the redraft. One of the skills of explanation writing is making sure that definitions fit smoothly into the whole text. For example: *Teeth... can be attacked... by bacteria. These tiny organisms...*

Sometimes the explanation of a fact involves describing an underlying process. Sometimes what has to be explained is itself a process. In both cases, the explanation needs to outline a process. The reader should be able to identify clear stages in this process, and to see what change is taking place within the overall process.

The four sections in the checklist will help the children to evaluate their partners' explanations, and to make suggestions for effective redrafting.

Group review

Children often struggle to see what they should improve in their own writing. However, by the age of 9–11, they should understand the importance of reflecting on a draft, deciding what can be improved in it and redrafting to produce a final version. These skills can be enhanced by group work in which the children discuss the improvements they could make to their own texts. This is self-assessment, but the group context encourages comparison and clear expression.

Working in groups of three, the children should review their explanation writing together. Each child can use an individual copy of page 32 to review all three texts. The sheet encourages the children to consider two specific features of their texts: whether the opening sentence prepares the reader for the rest of the text; and what connecting words (causal and/or temporal) they have used. In doing this, each child can compare his or her text with that of the other two children, which makes it easier to identify alterations that he or she could make to produce an improved final draft.

Read another

Read a friend's explanation.

What does it explain?

What specialist vocabulary is used?

Can you pick out three stages in the process
your friend has written about?

What is changed in this process?

Group review

Look at the three explanations your group have written.
Answer these questions for all three pieces of writing.

What opening sentences did you use?

What connecting words did you use?

What could you improve in each explanation?

17039